LONG ISLAND HERITAGE

THE G-5   1924-1955

BY RON ZIEL

RAILROAD HERITAGE PRESS
424 WEST 33 STREET   7TH FLOOR
NEW YORK, NY 10001   (212) CH 4-2100

ISBN 0-931584-05-1

ROBERT B. DUNNET

ART HUNEKE

LEFT: Bygone scenes of railroading as the engineer of a G-5 looks back from the cab for the conductor's "highball" signal. A quarter century has passed since this moment of departure from Woodside, in the Borough of Queens, New York City and so has steam, the open-window clerestory-roof coaches, the wooden platform, and the lampposts. ABOVE: The two longest-lived LIRR G-5 engines, Nos. 21 (31 years, 10 months service) and 24 (30 years, 10 months), rest out a weekend on the house tracks at Oyster Bay. Despite her age, the 24 is still not housebroken, having left a pile of iron horse manure in the form of firebox ashes on the track in front of her! BELOW: A pair of later G-5's, Nos. 39 and 50, the first and last of the dozen erected in 1929, face the water tower at Oyster Bay. In addition to marker lamps and small backup light, standard headlights were mounted on the tenders for night running in reverse. The roller bearing speed-control hookup applied to all LIRR locomotives after 1952 shows clearly on the tender truck journal box.

ROBERT B. DUNNET

CONTENTS

ACKNOWLEDGEMENTS

Even the publishing of a relatively small book requires the cooperation and assistance of collectors and historians to aid the author in completing the work with as much historical accuracy as possible. Most noteworthy of course are the photographers who contributed the pictures which they themselves shot between 1935 and 1955, or, in some instances, they had in their collections from other sources. Their credit lines appear with the pictures. John Krause assisted in photo selection and darkroom work, as well as editing. Dick Adams of the Pennsylvania Railroad Technical and Historical Society and Ed Crist supplied additional technical data. Besides furnishing photos, Art Huneke and Robert B. Dunnet also helped to piece together the last months of G-5 activity. My wife Elizabeth, being the administrator of The Steam Locomotive 39 Preservation Fund, has become intimately acquainted with the G-5's of late and was of great help in preparing the book. The principal source material was the author's previous work, *Steel Rails to the Sunrise* (co-authored with George H. Foster), and the feature article in the October, 1973 issue of *Trains* magazine by Bert Pennypacker.

RIGHT: In the mid-1930's a G-5 emerges from a wet snowfall at Central Islip as the gate tender waves to the engineer.

DEDICATION

To the volunteers, over 100 of whom are actively engaged in restoring the only surviving Long Island Rail Road steam locomotives, G-5's Nos. 35 and 39, to operation, this book is dedicated. They are the members of the Black River Volunteers Association and the Long Island-Sunrise Trail Chapter, National Railway Historical Society, working on No. 35, and the Steam Locomotive 39 Preservation Fund and Mainline Steam Foundation, rebuilding No. 39.

G. G. AYLING (ZIEL COLLECTION)

INTRODUCTION

In March of 1978 I was honored with a request that I write the introduction to this delightful book about the G-5. My long career with the Long Island Rail Road did not include working as a locomotive engineer, but as rules examiner during the latter part of World War II and immediately afterwards, I was fully qualified on air brakes and machinery and experienced a moderate amount of "running" with the G-5. This, combined with my overall love for railroading in general, I presume, sparked the author to call on me. It is a pleasure, I assure you; and the best way to introduce you to the remarkable dual-purpose G-5 is to relate a couple of heartwarming, firsthand experiences.

The G-5 was designed by the Pennsylvania Railroad as a dual-purpose locomotive for either local passenger or medium-tonnage freight trains, thus the 68-inch driving wheel diameter. In local passenger service it was designed to handle up to 10 cars; on the Long Island we abused that figure, handling 14 or 15 cars quite regularly. When we used the G-5 in freight service we often abused the intent of "medium tonnage" also. In both cases, the G-5 never let us down—it always performed the assigned task with aplomb! Accepted and proven steam locomotive practice was that the machine was "comfortably capable" of 1 mph of speed for each inch of driver diameter. This put the G-5 in a "comfortable" speed range of 70-odd mph, and at that speed they rode and steamed real well, that is if the "Pennsylvania real estate" we used for coal provided sufficient BTU's; too often, it didn't! On the Long Island we were blessed with a group of engineers, best left unnamed, known as "speed merchants" for their desire and ability to coax a G-5 well beyond this average. The fastest time that I ever clocked (with watch and mileposts, for our steam locomotives had no speed recorders) was on Train 38 across the Central branch between B Tower and Babylon. One of our high-wheeling speed merchants was making 81.5 mph; I assure you that a G-5 at that speed is *flying!*

Now farther afield than Long Island: Trenton, NJ and No. 27 fresh from an Altoona overhaul; pert, sassy, and apparently carefree on a delightful spring morning returning to the Long Island. The good old Pennsy would never let a buck slip by on a light engine move, so here she was in revenue service enroute to her homeland trailing 45 loads and a hack. I remember so well, accelerating—smart and snappy—through the middle track at Trenton station, just plain showing off her refurbishing, the valves set square and under the guiding hand of one of the masters of the art who like to "run 'em".

Back to the Long Island and Fremont Interlocking, where the New Haven joined us on their movements to and from the Bay Ridge float bridges in Brooklyn. On a rainy, nasty day No. 45 with 74 cars enroute from Holban Yard to Bay Ridge via the east leg of the Fresh Pond wye, stopped with the engine right smack on the crossovers in Fremont Interlocking so the rear end crew could realign the switches for the Montauk branch at Glendale. Think now of Rule 158: "Sand must not be used nor water allowed to run . . . . over the movable parts of interlockings". We just knew she'd have to cut and double—we *knew* it. But we didn't reckon on the combination of a master engineer with a master machine, for doggoned if the 45, properly coaxed and without any grit under her feet, didn't walk those 74 cars up the curved grade of the wye and happily off to Bay Ridge. It was something to see—memories are made of performances like this!

Wyandanch: World War II in progress and deadhead Pullman equipment heading east, enroute to Camp Upton to load up for a westbound "Main," a troop train heading west off the Island. Two G-5's with the lead engine being run by our congenial Road Foreman of Engines, Larry Stewart. He loved to run, so I would have no opportunity unless I rode the second engine. We had to stop at WK block limit signal to secure block authority to proceed, due to the local freight failing to clear in time for us to get our "K" card (clearance card) when we passed B Tower six miles back. My engineer, a true believer in "lubrication and a cool-running machine", had gone down on the ground to oil around while our conductor went to the block phone to get clearance. Having secured the block, the conductor threw us a highball and Larry whistled off. I quickly checked the left side where my engineer was still oiling around and he gave me a "G'wan, ya got it". So off we went. Larry moved out in a lackadaisical manner—surprising for him—not recalling for the moment that we were on close time to clear Ronkonkoma for the next westbound regular, and the dispatcher hadn't given us any help on him. I then committed the unpardonable sin: I latched out the throttle and "nudged" the boss! He leaned out the cab window, turned back and gave me a rather affronted look as I pointed to my watch and gave a full forward sweep of my arm, indicating "get going!" Meanwhile my engineer was having loud, unhappy, and profane cat-fits. "Good jumping Jehosaphat," he exclaimed, "don't ever do that to the boss! Now that wild-eyed bastard will fly. He's sorer'n'ell at being bumped!" Fly we did, much to my lad's unhappiness and I confess that I sure contributed my share of the flying.

And so I look back with a happy nostalgia and if I have been reasonably successful in what I set out to do, you will peruse this book with a better appreciation, perhaps, of the famous G-5 class and its capabilities; oftentimes they were astonishing, especially when handled by those men of the craft who had an understanding of and an appreciation for the steam locomotive.

Have a happy time of it!

W. S. Boerckel
May, 1978

W. S. BOERCKEL

W.S. Boerckel retired on June 1, 1978 as Supervising Operator—Maintenance of Way, after a 42-year career with the Long Island in which he gained extensive experience in all facets of steam, electric, and diesel operation. Generally acknowledged as one of the finest operating men in American railroading, Winfield "Winnie" Scott Boerckel is also a lifelong railfan and historian. As a young block operator in August of 1937, he took the accompanying photo of MR cabin at Manorville, with G-5 No. 41 about to leave the station pulling Train 211 from Greenport. OPPOSITE: Greatly underutilized, No. 38 deadheads a single coach over the Stony Brook Road bridge after dropping her train at the King's Park State Hospital in February of 1950.

JOHN KRAU

FOREWORD

By the early 1920's, the Pennsylvania Railroad needed a more powerful locomotive to operate its commuter services on the branchlines which ran up into the hills surrounding Pittsburgh. Normal practice would have been to downgrade older mainline passenger locomotives for this prosaic purpose, but the 1900-era D-class 4-4-0's and E-class 4-4-2's were already proving themselves incapable of handling the heavier trains and K-4 class 4-6-2's, still being built by the hundreds for the mainline limiteds, were hardly ready for downgrading—and wouldn't be for three decades! The Pennsy's great locomotive designer, William F. Kiesel Jr., decided on a solution which was probably unique in the history of American railroading; he laid out a brand-new locomotive, from the wheels up, intended specifically for rapid-acceleration commuter service.

Using the basic boiler of the E-6 4-4-2 and H-10 2-8-0 of the 1910-era, Kiesel adapted it to the 4-6-0 wheel arrangement, which itself had been virtually phased out of Class-one railroad designing offices years before. The result was the first G-5, No. 987, which rolled out of the PRR's sprawling Juniata Shops at Altoona, Pennsylvania, in June, 1923. Built on proven theory with known components, the new Ten-Wheeler required little testing and within four months, forty were in service, the vast majority sent to alleviate the Pittsburgh branchline crisis. The chunky 4-6-0, the biggest, heaviest and most modern of this wheel arrangement to get into production, outclassed many more modern 4-6-2 types and soon became known to PRR men as the "Pittsburgh Commuter Engine."

Meanwhile, the Long Island Rail Road, by this time both the biggest commuter conveyor in the USA and a subsidiary of the Pennsylvania, was in need of heavier motive power, as it was rapidly phasing out its fleet of wooden coaches, on its way to becoming the first all-steel car fleet operator in the U.S., in 1927. Naturally, the G-5 was the Long Island's answer. On the LIRR, however, the G-5 was to be the heaviest and most powerful passenger locomotive ever owned by that line, so the G-5's were initially classed with the highbrow title of "limited express service" and assigned to the long-distance (106 mi) Montauk trains, a job which they yielded to leased K-4 Pacifics, beginning in 1931.

By February of 1925, the Pennsylvania had built 90 G-5 engines for itself and in January of 1924, four were built for the LI, followed by five more in January of 1925, ten more in 1928, and a final dozen in 1929. This is the story of those 31 remarkable G-5 locomotives—Nos. 20 to 50—which served as the backbone of the motive power pool of the Long Island Rail Road through the Roaring '20's, the Great Depression, World War II, and the Korean conflict. "Pittsburgh Commuter Engine"—that was the G-5; but on the LIRR, Jamaica was her home and every day for three decades, thousands of passengers rode to and from their New York City jobs and their Long Island homes behind the tough, gutsy, and reliable Ten-Wheelers.

BELOW: No. 39 pops her safety valve at Ronkonkoma.

ART HUNEKE

BOYHOOD REMINISCENCES AND NO. 22

When the psychologists claim that early childhood experiences have a profound effect on the adult, often throughout his life, they are absolutely correct! A more apt example than the author of this monograph could not be found anywhere. As early as 1942, at age three, when my parents and I moved from New York City to Bellerose, not far from the LIRR Main Line and right across the road from the old Creedmoor Branch, I became personally acquainted with the steam locomotives of "the best railroad on Long Island." Through the 1940's my mother frequently took me—often accompanied by friends—down to the Bellerose or Queens Village stations to spend hours train-watching. During the last four years of the decade, my father would bring me to the Morris Park engine terminal once a year—the most exciting annual event, with the possible exception of Christmas, for a boy not yet at the age of ten, to be sure. Even more vivid than the G-5's are the memories of the C-51 0-8-0's and H-6sb 2-8-0's which worked the Creedmoor spur, and the leased Pennsy E-6 and K-4 speedsters that thundered down the Main near the Nassau County line, frequently at well over 70 mph. They shook even the heavy reinforced-concrete station platforms and doused us with soot. I was intimately familiar with the G-53 4-6-0's and H-10 2-8-0's as well, and have photos of me in engineer cap and carrying a toy lantern while standing on the pilot footboards to prove it!

Still, the G-5 played a central role in my formative years; the greatest thrill of the first decade of my life being when I not only rode the cab, but took the throttle of one of them on her break-in run at Richmond Hill after a major overhaul at Morris Park. Riding the engine on the turntable, taking sand, filling the tender with coal and water (the soaking wet coal chips flew all over the cab) and then sitting on the engineer's lap as he placed his heavy gauntlet-gloved hand on mine as we eased out the throttle... Memories formed in the mind of an eight-year-old that will last until my final hours, I am sure.

In 1949, we moved to Huntington on the Port Jefferson Branch where I would lean out the window of a coach and watch the doughty G-5 on the point as she assaulted the curving trackage of Cold Spring Hill. All too soon, the steam engines of my youth were gone and the G-5 was the last to go. By 1954, they were a rarity and the last one I ever saw was sooty and grimy as she sat on the New York Avenue bridge at Huntington station. I was walking to Junior High on a cold, clear winter morning and happened to look back as the dirty old G-5 halted on the bridge, steam seeming to ooze from every pore. I paused and watched as she worked the long commuter train out of the station and I knew how uncommon the sight had become. I was never to see it again.

-Ron Ziel   President, Steam Locomotive 39 Preservation Fund

JOHN KRAUSE

ABOVE LEFT: In 1948, on one of the many train-watching forays to the old Bellerose station, I took the first photo of my life, of my mother and my railfan neighbor, Edward Regan. They wondered why I waited and I said "I want a train in the picture". Several m.u. electrics passed, but I insisted on a *steam* train. When no westbound showed, I looked over my shoulder and saw the fury of a steamer bellowing through Queens Village, a mile or so behind me. This was the result: a blurry box camera shot with a G-5 roaring by in the background; the first of many thousands of pictures I was to take, including more than 15,000 photos of steam locomotives in over forty countries. ABOVE RIGHT: A few minutes later, another G-5—No. 22—blasted through westbound and my mother took this photo as I watched the big 4-6-0. LEFT: At about the same time, on May 22, 1948, No. 22 sits on track 8 at Jamaica station with an eastbound train. In the background is Krug's bakery. When the wind was right, the aroma of fresh-baked bread mingled with the smells of hot valve oil and soft coal smoke at Jamaica station and a young boy on the platform experienced his first preconception of paradise...

G-5 DOUBLEHEADERS

If one steam locomotive, blasting down the main with a string of tuscan red coaches behind was awesome to behold, a pair of them on the head end was even more sensational and the Long Island Rail Road frequently indulged in doubleheading. Certain trains were pulled by two engines to Manorville, where one took part of the consist down the branch to the Montauk Division and the other continued with the remainder of the train to Greenport. Sometimes a particularly popular train, especially on summer weekends, grew too heavy for one locomotive to keep the schedule, so a second was added. Occasionally when motive power was required at one of the eastern terminals (again, chiefly on summer weekends) a second engine was coupled to a regular train, rather than run out light. Of course, a malfunction on one engine could result in another coupling on ahead to assist the crippled one. During the "Standard Era," when the Pennsylvania Railroad's designs dominated the motive power roster of the LIRR for 30 years, beginning about 1925, G-5's were frequently doubleheaded with Pennsy E and K classes as well as with

F. G. ZAHN

themselves. Sometimes, an H class freight hog even got into the act. LEFT: When the G-5 was still in her infancy, No. 32, just eleven months old and No. 41, less than two months old, doublehead Train No. 12, the summer Saturdays-only *Shinnecock Express*, through Mineola on August 31, 1929. LOWER LEFT: Another tandem show as two "Big G's" pull a train out of the Richmond Hill Storage Yard in 1949. RIGHT: A similar scene, two years earlier. BELOW: The last known steam doubleheader occurred when the air pump on No. 35 malfunctioned and No. 21 was sent to bring her in. The tender lettering of both engines is the same style, but the spacing is different. The scene is Floral Park on November 11, 1954—less than a year before the end of steam on the LIRR. The choice of numbers 20 thru 50 for the 31 G-5 class locomotives was in deference to keeping the numbers as low as possible and when the G-5 began arriving on Long Island, a magnificent series of camelback 4-4-2's (Nos. 1-4) and 4-6-0's (Nos. 5-19), built by Baldwin (1901-03), were still very active, so the new engines followed in sequence.

RON ZIEL COLLECTION

F. G. ZAHN

G-5 AND PENNSY DOUBLEHEADING

The most frequent of doubleheading combinations on the LIRR during the 1930's and '40's saw a 68-inch driving wheeled G-5 coupled ahead of a leased 80-inch drivered E-6 or K-4. Between 1929 and 1949, twenty-six of the eighty-three E-6 Atlantics saw service on the LIRR and seventy-one of the 425 K-4 Pacifics were leased during the 1931-1951 period. An appreciable number of older E-3, E-7, K-2 and K-3 passenger engines, as well as B-6 and B-8 0-6-0 switchers and H-6, H-8 and H-9 2-8-0 freight locomotives, were also on the LIRR at the time. RIGHT: Eastbound at Union Hall Street, Jamaica, G-5 No. 29 and an E-6 combine to produce a cloud of white exhaust in 1946. BELOW: No. 38 and K-4 No. 5406 with Train No. 12 at Bethpage a decade earlier. At this time, most Long Island G-5 engines possessed the 110P82 tender, virtually identical to those used by the PRR on its K-4's assigned to long-distance service, while the Long Island-assigned K-4 engines had much smaller tenders, as this photo clearly shows. The net effect when doubleheading was to make both locomotives appear similar in size! No. 5406 was to become the LI's "own" K-4, having been assigned to LIRR work almost constantly during the two decades in which these magnificent thoroughbreds worked the heaviest of LIRR trains. Indeed, the 5406, built in 1928 and retired in 1957, apparently ran more miles on Long Island than she did on the Pennsylvania!

F. R. DIRKES

F. R. DIRKES

GEORGE E. VOTAVA

ROBERT F. COLLINS

G-5 AND PENNSY POWER AT TERMINALS

The Pennsylvania and Long Island locomotives often mingled rather freely at the major engine terminals of Morris Park, Port Jefferson, Greenport, Ronkonkoma, Oyster Bay and Montauk. UPPER LEFT: August 8, 1949 finds LI G-5 engines and PRR K-4 types waiting to take out the evening "commutes" at Morris Park. LEFT: Two E-3 Atlantics flank a pair of LI G-5's at Oyster Bay in the late 1930's. At least sixteen of the trim little 4-4-2's and thirty-one similar E-7 Atlantics were used on Long Island from the late '20's until the early '40's, pulling light Oyster Bay and other branch trains, extras, work trains and they even handled the renowned little two-car local that made a round-trip daily between Amagansett and Greenport, via the Manorville Branch. The "Scoot," or "Cape Horn Train," as it was known, was taken off the timetable in 1931.

ART HUNEKE

PENNSY G-5's ON LONG ISLAND

Although only ten of the 90 Pennsylvania G-5 engines are known to have run on Long Island, their time span is greater than any other class, having been on the LIRR as early as 1928 and as late as 1955! That their use on the LIRR was of minor consequence is evidenced by the fact that very few pictures of them on the Island are available. The ten Pennsy Ten-Wheelers known to have been leased to the LIRR (mostly during the immediate post-World War II years) were Nos. 1589, 1961, 5703, 5704, 5706, 5707, 5714, 5717, 5724 and 5741. The latter locomotive, No. 5741, presents one of the greatest locomotive mysteries in the entire history of the Long Island Rail Road. With the LIRR rapidly dieselizing, the last of the leased PRR engines—four K-4 Pacifics—were returned to the mother road in October, 1951. In the remaining four years of steam operation, the LIRR had ample power and G-5 and H-10 locomotives were dispatched to the scrap yards soon after retirement, due to high prevailing scrap prices during the Korean War. By September, 1955, the last full month of steam operation, just seven G-5's were left on the roster and it is doubtful if all of these were still serviceable, while the last three H-10 2-8-0's were retired that month. Yet, there was the 5741, sporting a Long Island tender no less, steamed up at Morris Park, working in Holban Yard and even running the Babylon-Patchogue local service for one day when a diesel broke down! She was only on the LIRR for a week—two, at most—under totally mysterious circumstances and only one photographer is known to have gotten her on film. RIGHT: With her "K-4" LIRR tender, PRR No. 5741 is shown at Holban in September, 1955 in a print made from a color transparency. Coincidentally, she was to become the only preserved PRR G-5 and can be seen, with a low 70P82A tender, at the State Railroad Museum in Strasburg, Pennsylvania.

FREIGHT HAULING G-5's

Although renowned as a rapid-acceleration and quick-stopping local passenger locomotive, the G-5 was a true dual-service machine and could really take a medium-tonnage freight in tow. Through a ridiculous quirk in the Federal laws, the G-5 fleet never received automatic stokers, although the H-10, with virtually the same boiler, did. Like so many bureaucratic monsters, the law was not based on a sensible criteria, such as the amount of coal consumed in a high-capacity boiler, or the fact that the G-5 not only lacked a trailing truck, but the wide spacing between the main and rear driving axles made the locomotive extremely rough-riding at speed, but rather the decision was based on the weight on driving wheels! The H-10, with four driving axles, was slightly over the limit, the G-5 with three driving axles, was under. A result was that although a relatively small locomotive by mainline standards, the G-5 often carried two firemen in freight service. Although all 31 G-5's were used in freight service occasionally, two seemed to have been called for this work more often than the others. LEFT: No. 25 trundles a freight through Bellaire in 1949. BELOW: No. 45 climbs the grade at Mill Neck on March 20, 1950.

F. G. ZAHN

JOHN KRAUSE

12

ART HUNEKE

LEFT: As late as midsummer of 1955, a diesel breakdown at Mineola brought out a G-5 to assist with freight tonnage. No. 38 pulls diesel No. 464 and its train through the rain at the Roslyn Road crossing. BELOW: More "medium tonnage" G-5 freight action right at mid-century as No. 39 brings about fifteen cars through Merillon Avenue in a flying meet with No. 32 on a passenger train and No. 42 does likewise at Bellaire in 1950. No. 42 has a sheet-metal covering over her strap-steel pilot, an LIRR device for fending off snow which was applied to leased PRR power as well. The final regular service run of a G-5 occurred on Tuesday, October 11, 1955, when No. 50 briefly handled a work train out of Jamaica.

F. G. ZAHN

F. G. ZAHN

Oyster Bay, the favorite engine photographer's weekend haunt during the G-5 era. ABOVE: No. 21 faces the relatively new (c. 1940) water tower. BELOW: No. 35 and sister 38 coexist with a 1951-built Fairbanks-Morse 1600 horsepower diesel.

"JUST A LITTLE LONGER THAN INSTANTLY"

Remember the Pennsy's concept of a 4-6-0...the G-5? I do. Anyone who ever lived within the limits of Long Island's "Commuter Country" back when steam took 'em to work in the AM and brought 'em home at night, will remember this PRR breed of Ten-Wheeler as the 'dragster' of the railroad world! For those readers who never knew the G-5...here is what you missed.

I was fortunate to have lived for several years in a town that provided not one, but two stages on which the Long Island's G-5's performed with remarkable talent. The town was Farmingdale; Stage No. 1 was the station serving the town proper, situated on the north and on the Main Line. Stage No. 2 was a smaller affair at the south end, located on the Central Branch. We lived between the two lines and my ears, during the morning and evening commuter periods, were constantly tuned in on both. What a program THAT was!

Everyone has their own special way of remembering certain locomotives of the steam era. I remember the G-5 for the way it sounded leaving a station from a standing start. One would find himself swearing that what he heard was not possible! The G-5 sounded normal for maybe the first four barks of the 4-beat exhaust rhythm. But, from that point on you KNEW it was a G-5! That measured series of individual exhausts would build to a continuous staccato so rapidly that it could only be described as "just a little longer than INSTANTLY!" And...this was with a long string of coaches jam-packed with commuters yet!

In the morning it would be a steady parade westbound in and out of the Main Line station as the G-5's in rapid-fire order were shot out of the cannon at Ronkonkoma, turnaround point for commuter traffic on the Main Line. The smaller South Farmingdale station, though not as busy, also rang with the sound of G-5's that had come barreling up the single track of the Central Branch from Babylon, the point at which they had swung northwestward off the Montauk Branch after starting their runs at Speonk, commuter turnaround point on that route.

Interspersed with the G-5 "talk" would be the sounds of an occasional E-6 Atlantic, or more often one of the big K-4 Pacifics, the engine for which I shall always be indebted to the Pennsy for designing. The G-5 never failed to identify itself however, within seconds after the engineman placed his hand on the throttle! This entire parade would be repeated in the opposite direction each evening. After a "hard day at the office," the G-5's would be bringing 'em back to hearth and home.

Steam is now long gone on Long Island. The commuters at first felt the smooth tug of Fairbanks-Morse diesels along with a handful of Alco RS-1's. Then they were riding behind RS-3's and Century 420's, followed by General Motors GP-38's. Soon, they will be traveling "to and from" in spanking new high speed equipment, thanks to the Metropolitan Transportation Authority. I'm all for this—intelligent progress is of the utmost importance to today's railroads. But I can't help wondering how many of the older commuters realize that they were once privileged to ride behind what was probably the greatest engine ever designed to haul their kind of train: the big, Belpaire-boilered Ten-Wheeler known as a G-5, the engine that took "just a little longer than INSTANTLY" to get cracking!

—J. P. Krzenski

Jules P. Krzenski was raised in Southampton, where he photographed H-10 and K-4 engines while still in high school in the late 1940's, but never the G-5's, whose runs terminated at Speonk; they rarely ventured east of there after about 1931. It was after he moved to Farmingdale, that he came to know the G-5 first-hand. RIGHT: Beneath a panoply of fleecy billows, No. 26 speeds a baggage car, combine and four coaches that is the consist of Train 625, near Syosset, en route from Port Jefferson to Jamaica in the late 1930's.

UNSCHEDULED MEET AT HUNTINGTON

August 6, 1950 saw G-5 No. 29 racing eastbound toward Huntington in the late afternoon with a local passenger train (ABOVE: at Mineola in 1948) while H-10 No. 101 (BELOW: at Kings Park in 1949) was coming west with the freight from Port Jefferson. After clearing the main track, 101 was switching a siding when a novice brakeman threw the switch just as the passenger train arrived on the scene at 50 miles per hour, resulting in a classic pile-up (RIGHT) which attracted hundreds of spectators.

RON ZIEL COLLECTION

RON ZIEL COLLECTION

F. G. ZAHN

The freight brakeman, on the job just a few weeks, had misunderstood a hand signal from the conductor and No. 29 barrelled right into the siding, slamming into a steel Nickel Plate Road boxcar with an explosive crash that was heard several miles away. ABOVE: The wrecking crew begins the clean-up task. ABOVE RIGHT: A wooden Jersey Central boxcar was reduced to splinters; what little remained of it was wrapped around the smokebox of No. 101. Although over 50 people were injured, there were no deaths; a fact partly attributable to the wooden car acting as a shock absorber. This was the last LIRR wreck involving two steam locomotives. At this time there was an influx of diesels and both 29 and 101 were scrapped, although the latter engine apparently suffered only minor damage. RIGHT: Begrimed and filthy G-5 No. 45 is shown the following day with a trainload of ballast to repair the right-of-way. Since she too was retired in August, 1950, this may well have been the last run she ever made; an ignominious and humble ending, the antithesis of the spectacular manner in which sister No. 29 had careened into oblivion the day before!

SERVICING AND REBUILDING THE G-5's

Although locomotives were normally seen hard at work, they spent much of their careers simmering quietly in the roundhouse, or on terminal tracks, or in the shops for every class of maintenance from monthly boiler washes to complete rebuildings. The G-5 was no exception to this rule and although the LIRR had photographs of the shops in their files at one time, none have survived and the only known pictures of G-5 engines under these circumstances are shown here. With just a year of steam operation left, a G-5—believed to be either No. 38 or No. 50—was completely overhauled in the fall of 1954, including new firebox sheets, staybolts and boiler tubes. When retired, she was still good for at least four years of service, but LIRR President Thomas M. Goodfellow, ignoring the pleas of railway enthusiasts and his own middle-management people, ordered her scrapped, dismissing the idea that the public would ever be interested in steam excursions! LEFT and RIGHT: Firebox and smokebox views of the last steam locomotive ever to receive a class-five overhaul at Morris Park. LOWER LEFT: A pair of G-5 locomotives, displaced to one end of the roundhouse by the conquering diesel host, simmer quietly between calls to duty as a machinist repairs a part of the smoke box of the rearmost engine.

HICKSVILLE PROTECT ENGINE

In a daily ritual of many years standing, the LIRR would dispatch a light engine to Hicksville early each morning, where she would take up a position on the east leg of the wye in anticipation of a possible breakdown of one of the commuter trains. After the morning rush, the engine would return to Morris Park, then go back out to Hicksville in the late afternoon to cover the eastbound return of the commuters. Usually this was the most uneventful assignment an engine crew could get, but periodic breakdowns, such as those on pages 9 and 13, rendered the Hicksville protect engine an important assignment. RIGHT: In later years, No. 21 frequently drew this chore and she is shown in the typical filthy demeanor of steam in its full decline, positioned on the wye at Hicksville on a cloudy, gray November 8, 1954.

ART HUNEKE

ART HUNEKE

G-5 ENTHUSIAST EXCURSIONS

Despite Tom Goodfellow's derisive comment; "Who the hell would want to ride behind one of those things?", when it was suggested that he retain one or two steam locomotives for excursion use after the 1955 dieselization, the G-5 had already established herself as a popular fan-tripper, attracting hundreds of passengers to each of several successful excursions during the final year of steam operations. LOWER LEFT: No. 50, the newest steam engine built for the LIRR, is surrounded by her admirers in the Bay Ridge, Brooklyn, yard on October 31, 1954. ABOVE: No. 39 powered the last steam-hauled passenger train ever to operate into the original terminal of the Mainline at Greenport, where she is shown taking coal and being turned on June 5, 1955. LOWER RIGHT: The dubious honor of winding up 119 years of steam operation on the Long Island Rail Road fell to G-5 No. 35, shown pulling the last steam train—another railfan special—past the St. James station on October 16, 1955.

VINCENT F. SEYFRIED

JOHN KRAUSE

LEFT: No. 20, first of the Long Island G-5 4-6-0's, is shown in her original livery, including gold striping, and pulling a small, class 70P82, tender at Long Island City in the 1920's. Behind her is a D-56 class 4-4-0, No. 82, fitted with an experimental feedwater heater.

BELOW: No. 20 is pulling into the station at Ronkonkoma under the scrutiny of a young boy in 1950. A point of extreme trivia for the connoisseur of the G-5: the semicircular grab iron on the smokebox front was generally mounted above the door on the early engines (Nos. 20-28) which possessed pilot-mounted air reservoirs. As built, Nos. 20-24 apparently had the grab iron mounted below. This was later reversed on all of the early G-5's, but No. 20 was back to the original position by 1948, as evidenced by the photos on this page and the front cover; the only engine to have this abnormality.

Construction date	Number	Retired
January, 1924	3851	January, 1951

HAROLD K. VOLLRATH

THE COMPLETE FLEET: NO. 20 - NO. 50

F. G. ZAHN

LEFT and ABOVE: No. 21 is shown at Long Island City in 1927 when she was assigned to the LIRR's premier train, No. 18, *The Sunrise Special* and sported a magnificent emblem in the process. No. 21 went to the scrapper in 1955 but this tender is preserved, along with engine No. 35. BELOW: Although 31½ years old and just four months from retirement, the old girl romps through Hicksville in this scene of panned-motion with all the vigor of her youthful days when she ran *The Sunrise Special* from Long Island City to Montauk in less than three hours.

Construction date	Number	Retired
January, 1924	3853	October, 1955

The technique of night photography of locomotives, using a combination of flash bulbs and available light, or multible bulbs ("painting with light") while the tripod-mounted camera makes a long exposure of a minute or more, is relatively new. It was pioneered by such renowned photographers as Don Wood during the late 1950's—too late to have been used on Long Island in steam days. In the ensuing two decades, many railway photographers, including the author of this monograph, have utilized the technique on steam engines in 50 countries around the world. While other photographers were busy chasing the last steam locomotives on Long Island in the early 1950's, Richard B. Wettereau and Robert Viken shot nearly 200 4" x 5" negatives of the old stations—half of them at night with fill-in flash. On September 25, 1952, the night they were "bulbing" the Oyster Bay station, they went into the yard and got this spectacular photograph of a pair of G-5's and a pair of diesels, with No. 22 in the foreground. This is the only known picture taken of an LIRR steam scene using this technique. Unfortunately, despite the stunning success of their first attempt, Viken and Wettereau never repeated the feat in the remaining three years of LI steam operations.

Construction date	Number	Retired
January, 1924	3854	July, 1955

HARRY J. TREDE

HAROLD K. VOLLRATH

LEFT: No. 23 simmers patiently between assignments at Oyster Bay on April 10, 1938. ABOVE: Nine years later, with cab curtains flapping and a critical fireman peering from the cab, she rolls through New Hyde Park, as the semaphore blade behind her drops to mark her passing. The assignment of three various types of tenders to the G-5 class is another confusing issue. Apparently, several of the earliest engines came with the small 70P82 variety (page 20) and some with the enlarged 70P82A (LEFT), here, but by 1927, the larger 110P82A (ABOVE) was already in evidence. The 70P82's were rebuilt into the 70P82A type and some of them wound up in work train service. The twenty-two latter G-5's, delivered in 1928-29, all had 110P82A tenders. All 90 of the Pennsylvania G-5 engines trailed the smaller tenders. The 70P82 held 16 tons of coal and 7700 gallons of water, the 70P82A carried 12 tons and 8300 gallons and the 110P82A had a capacity of 14½ tons and 12,730 gallons.

Construction date	Number	Retired
February, 1924	3855	June, 1950

23

UPPER LEFT: No. 24, photographed from BJ Tower in Babylon, backs down through the yard shortly after electrification reached there in 1925. ABOVE: Another view from above shows No. 24 pulling away from beneath the Mineola Avenue overpass. LOWER LEFT: 24 and 39 at Oyster Bay, Memorial Day, 1955. BELOW: While a diesel with a local freight waits on the siding, No. 24, the last G-5 to retain the original big headlight, highballs through Mineola with Train No. 635 from Port Jefferson.

Construction date	Number	Retired
January, 1925	3973	October, 1955

RON ZIEL COLLECTION

GEORGE E. VOTAVA

ABOVE: Few photos are as expressive of the stubby and squat, yet racy "bulldog" demeanor of the G-5 as this one, taken at Jamaica in the 1930's. LEFT: With B Tower along the tracks in the background, No. 25 brings Train No. 4226, the Central Islip to Jamaica Sunday-only accommodation, along the Main Line. Taken from an overpass of the famous Vanderbilt Motor Parkway, this photo shows many aspects of the LIRR long gone, including the outhouse and the diamond-shaped crossing sign. By 1920, there were almost 1000 of these signs guarding the grade crossings of the LIRR; just four are known to remain—two fo them in the author's garage! Train 4226 returned visitors from the State Mental Hospital at Central Islip. For decades, the LIRR ran such Sunday trains to the hospitals at Brentwood, Central Islip, Kings Park and, long ago, to Creedmoor. Slowly, this service also vanished, the last hospital trains being withdrawn from the Pilgrim State Hospital run in May, 1978.

Construction date	Number	Retired
January, 1925	3974	November, 1951

ROBERT B. DUNNET

ROBERT F. COLLINS

JOHN KRAUSE

ABOVE: A scant six months before she was scrapped, a shiny and sprightly No. 26 pulled a commuter train up Roslyn Hill on May 14, 1951. The club car behind the tender, No. 811, was leased to a group of affluent commuters on the Oyster Bay branch; they paid extra for the comfort of this air-conditioned service as part of the regular consist of their train. Similar arrangements were made on other branches. UPPER RIGHT: No. 26 drifted past Dunton Tower and a DD-1 electric locomotive, fresh out of the shops in 1938. RIGHT: Waiting passengers step back respectfully on the platform as a dirty-faced 26 pulls into Mineola on May 22, 1948.

Construction date	Number	Retired
January, 1925	3975	November, 1951

ABOVE: In a panoramic view, No. 27 sweeps around the curve at Mill Neck on February 6, 1949. LEFT: She is shown at Richmond Hill, eleven years earlier. Here again, the sheet-metal snow shield is seen to be an on-again, off-again device; often being removed from a locomotive during the winter, while being left in place all summer long. This was another little way in which the LIRR violated the exacting standards by which the Pennsylvania Railroad ran all of its operations; PRR locomotives never carried snow shields. As a further minor act of rebellion, LIRR men often affixed the shields to the pilots of leased Pennsy E and K class engines. Another bit of individuality was the painting of the smokebox doors black. Set in the middle of the graphite smokebox front, with the number plate mounted on the door, this presented a handsome appearance. Although the LIRR stopped painting the doors of its locomotives black during World War II, the scheme was still applied to leased PRR K-4 engines as late as 1951! No. 27 was one of eleven G-5's—more than one-third of the roster—to be retired, in November, 1951, along with two H-10 2-8-0's and following the return of the last four K-4's to the PRR the previous month. New diesels were arriving at a rapid pace in 1951 and scrap was at a premium, hence the great wipe-out of the LIRR steam roster at that time.

Construction date	Number	Retired
January, 1925	3976	November, 1951

HAROLD K. VOLLRATH

JOHN KRAUSE

F. G. ZAHN

ABOVE LEFT: Resembling two pigs at a trough, G-5 No. 28 and H-10 No. 107 stand side-by-side at Port Jefferson in 1951, in a scene which offers a good comparison of the tenders of both classes. ABOVE: On a cold March morning in 1954, No. 28 brings a westbound commuter local into Huntington station. BELOW: She is coupled to her evening commuter train at the Long Island City terminal in May, 1946.

Construction date	Number	Retired
January, 1925	3975	July, 1955

LEFT and RIGHT: No. 29 on the turntable and pulling up to the watering column as she is serviced between runs at Oyster Bay on August 12, 1948. BELOW: On October 9, 1938, No. 29 pulled the last revenue train to Wading River, before that branch was cut back to its pre-1895 terminus of Port Jefferson. Here, block-operator W. S. Boerckel is shaking hands with the crew of two enginemen, conductor and two brakemen, just after their arrival at Wading River. Note that the last twenty-two G-5 engines beginning with No. 29, had no air reservoir on the pilot, as the first nine had. On these later engines, it was re-positioned behind the cylinder saddle. Among the ninety PRR G-5's, there was no pattern to this phenomenon; some had the tank in front, others did not. Quite frequently, certain engines were associated with certain branches or runs and No. 29 was a Port Jefferson Branch meanderer for much of her career. Twelve years after the termination of Wading River service, she met her sensational fate at Huntiongton station, the only LIRR G-5 to be scrapped because of a wreck.

Construction date	Number	Retired
September, 1928	4195	August, 1950

ABOVE LEFT: Fireman Bill Aha and Engineer Fred Shiertcliff pose alongside the brand-new No. 30 at Morris Park in 1928. In the background is the gas car which ran the local Sag Harbor Branch service from Bridgehampton.
ABOVE RIGHT: No. 30 is flanked by sister 24 and a smaller, older 4-6-0, G-53 No. 141 (built by Brooks in 1917) at Oyster Bay, circa 1937.
BELOW: On Abraham Lincoln's birthday in 1949, No. 30 rolled through Stony Brook.

Construction date	Number	Retired
September, 1928	4196	June, 1951

F. R. DIRKES

F. G. ZAHN

ABOVE: Roaring out from under the Vanderbilt Motor Parkway bridge at Bethpage, G-5 No. 31 brings a Railway Post Office car, two baggage cars and three coaches, the consist of Train No. 204, *The Greenport Express,* enroute to the namesake terminal of the Mainline, which opened for service in 1844. Ninety-seven years later, when this photograph was taken, steam was still the absolute ruler beyond electrified territory, but a decade later the diesels were rapidly taking over. LEFT: No. 31 drifts by Dunton Tower on her way back to the engine terminal after bringing a train into Jamaica from the east.

Construction date	Number	Retired
September, 1928	4197	November, 1951

F. R. DIRKES

The Long Island Rail Road was originally built through the scrub pine barrens along the middle of Long Island, as a link in a rail-boat-rail route between New York and Boston. As such, it was not designed to serve the local needs of the area it traversed. By 1850, just six years after the 96-mile mainline from Brooklyn to Greenport was opened, the New York, New Haven & Hartford line was completed across southern Connecticut, dooming the lucrative New York-Boston trade for the LIRR. Settling down as a local system, the LIRR tried to develop the pine barrens, with limited success. ABOVE: 90 years after the failure of the Boston route, No. 32 traversed the bleak, endless flats at Brentwood, through scenery that had changed little since the tracks were laid through there in 1843. After World War II, suburban sprawl enveloped the area and scenes such as this are now to be found only east of Medford on the Main Line and Patchogue on the Montauk Branch. RIGHT: No. 32 is the picture of reliability as she shrugs off a heavy snowfall near St. James in 1950.

Construction date	Number	Retired
September, 1928	4198	October, 1955

JOHN KRAUSE

F. R. DIRKES

JOHN KRAUSE

F. G. ZAHN

UPPER LEFT: Back in the 1930's, the LIRR made a good effort to keep even its steam locomotives clean and presentable; No. 33 is getting a washdown with steaming hot water after coming into the Morris Park terminal. A more elaborate steam and oil-cleaning gun was frequently employed to rid the motive power of road grime. LOWER LEFT: No. 33 at Port Jefferson in 1949. BELOW: The following year, the hefty 4-6-0 worked ten coaches up Mount Olivet, towards Fresh Pond from Long Island City. The Bushwick Branch curves off to the left.

Construction date	Number	Retired
September, 1928	4199	November, 1951

F. R. DIRKES

When the railroads dieselized, they not only failed to acknowledge the vital role played by the passing steam locomotive in developing their great transportation systems, but for some inexplicable reason, they chose to disparage steam and all it had accomplished. The Long Island Rail Road unfortunately was part of the pro-diesel, anti-steam nonsense and issued some downright ridiculous press releases in comparing the vaunted new diesel technology with the "outmoded" and "obsolete" steam locomotive. In 1959, four years after the last G-5's were retired, the Goodfellow administration, which was expert on public relations pablum, but naive on the facts of motive power capabilities, published a 125th anniversary booklet which showed a photograph of a 2400 horsepower Fairbanks-Morse diesel with the following caption: "Trains like this have as many as seventeen cars today. The old steamers could seldom

handle more than seven or eight." Needless to say, the booklet did not show the photo of No. 34 (ABOVE) pulling eleven cars, nine of which are Pennsylvania P-70 heavyweight coaches. The "seventeen" referred to in the LIRR publication were lightweight LIRR P-54 cars, twenty of which couldn't slow a K-4 down to 60 mph! This photo was taken in 1941, a few months prior to the Japanese attack on Pearl Harbor, but after the old World War I Army training base at Camp Upton near Yaphank on the Main Line had been reactivated as a reception center. The G-5's handled many troop extras at that time, including entire trains that had come from the mainland through Penn Station in New York. This train is at Bethpage, bound from Upton to New York. RIGHT: Just after World War II, the 34 blasted through Floral Park at high speed, her canvas curtains flapping out of the back of the cab on a sub-freezing winter's day.

Construction date	Number	Retired
September, 1928	4200	November, 1951

F. R. DIRKES

A story told by LIRR old-timers goes that one day, three or four decades ago, the hostler at Speonk was telling a train crewman that a locomotive in the yard was carrying the train number on her smokebox. The trainman, apparently with visions of big train numberboards á la Union Pacific mounted on a Long Island engine, wagered $5 that the hostler had been hitting the bar at the Speonk Inn too heavily. When they walked to the west end of the yard to settle the debate, there was G-5 No. 35, coupled to Train No. 35 and ready to head out to Jamaica! The hostler rubbed salt in the wound by polishing up No. 35's number plate, as the trainman pulled a fiver out of his wallet. ABOVE and RIGHT: The trim Ten-Wheeler is shown at Morris Park on the servicing tracks in the mid-1930's and facing the concrete coal tipple from one of the turntable tracks in 1952. BELOW: Again in 1952, 35 is performing in spectacular blurred motion, bringing a morning commuter train through Floral Park. For twenty-two years following her retirement, No. 35, along with the *Sunrise Special* tender which originally served No. 21, was displayed in Eisenhower Park, near East Meadow. She is being prepared to be moved to the Black River & Wester Railroad in New Jersey, to be rebuilt for operation on that shortline.

Construction date	Number	Retired
September, 1928	4201	October, 1955

F. G. ZAHN (ZIEL COLLECTION)

FRED CALLAN (ZIEL COLLECTION)

BELOW: Forty years ago, a young block operator named W. S. Boerckel handed orders up to the fireman of G-5 No. 36 as she rolled out of the setting sun and through Deer Park station. LEFT: On December 27, 1947, at the peak of the Great Blizzard, the big Ten-Wheeler, piled high with snow, brought an eastbound train through Union Hall Street. No. 36 was the first G-5 to be dispatched to the scrap dealer, in April, 1950, but this is the latest known photo of her under steam, so it is possible that she saw active service for just twenty years—or less—then was held in storage to be cannibalized for spare parts.

Construction date	Number	Retired
October, 1928	4202	April, 1950

JOHN KRAUSE

F. R. DIRKES

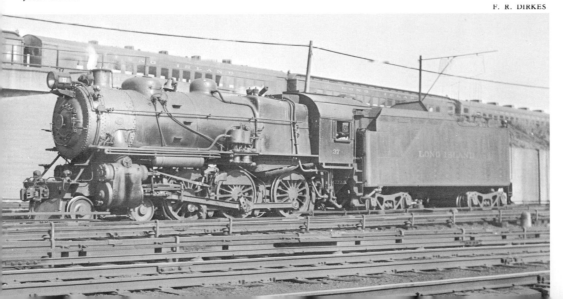

LEFT: No. 37 heading into the engine terminal at Morris Park on February 13, 1937. ABOVE: She is shown trundling down the Port Jefferson Branch with one coach, east of Kings Park, on February 26, 1950. The practice with the Sunday-only visitors' train to Kings Park State Hospital was to bring the train onto the hospital siding, then the locomotive (virtually always a G-5, although a K-4 occasionally drew the assignment) and one coach for extra braking power would run up to Port Jefferson to turn on the wye. When the passengers returned to their cars, the locomotive was back where she belonged—at the west end of the train ready to return them to Jamaica.

Construction date	Number	Retired
October, 1928	4203	November, 1951

JOHN KRAUSE

F. R. DIRKES

ART HUNEKE

From the earliest history of the Long Island Rail Road, it served the various horseracing tracks along its lines, operating special trains for the spectators and hauling in the nags in their own private cars. ABOVE: Although horse car moves, which normally consisted of only one or two cars, almost always drew a smaller locomotive (in the latter steam era, usually a G-53 4-6-0), on May 22, 1948 a burly G-5, No. 38, brought a pair of Horse Pullmans through Mineola. UPPER RIGHT: The 38 worked a three-car local at Glen Cove on December 26, 1939. RIGHT: Toward the end of her career, in the summer of 1955, a very grimy No. 38 dragged a lame diesel and twenty-odd cars of freight through Mineola. When sister 39 was put on display in 1956, she carried the number plate shown here on 38, since Tom Goodfellow, in yet another public relations gambit, had given the keystone plate from No. 39 to Brooklyn Dodgers baseball catcher Roy Campanella, whose uniform carried the same number. No. 39 (and 38) had been retired the very week that the Dodgers won the World Series and Campanella was a railfan of sorts, so the award was timely; putting No. 38's plate on the 39 definitely was not!

Construction date	Number	Retired
October, 1928	4204	October, 1955

LEFT: From an unusual high front angle, No. 39 was photographed at Mineola station, from the Mineola Avenue overpass on March 11, 1935. ABOVE: The big Ten-Wheeler with an excursion train at Mattituck on June 5, 1955. Although the G-5 engines ran out of Greenport and Speonk as late as 1951 on a regular basis, there are incredibly few photographs of them on Long Island's East End, hence the use of a railfan trip photo here. There are literally hundreds of photographs taken of the G-5's at such terminals as Oyster Bay, Port Jefferson, and Ronkonkoma, but just a few regular-service pictures survive from Greenport and only one solitary photo from Speonk (P. 50), which is just thirty miles beyond Ronkonkoma! In fact, fewer than a dozen photos of G-5's between Babylon and Montauk are available; less than the number a photographer such as Dunnet or Huneke or Krause may have taken at Oyster Bay in one day! During the 1920's and 1930's, when the G-5's held down Montauk runs, nobody seemed to be on hand to photograph them—except for a few enthusiasts who rode Sunday excursion trains to the easternmost terminal and took a few photos in the yard. The situation on the mainline east of Ronkonkoma is almost as sparse; most of the known photos of G-5's on regular trains in that area are reproduced in this book. RIGHT: Robert B. Dunnet, formerly a fireman on Pennsylvania Railroad steam locomotives and more recently

LIRR Yardmaster at Holban Yard, is shown at the throttle of No. 39 in the summer of 1955. No. 39 was donated to The Museums At Stony Brook, where she was placed on display in June, 1956. In the late 1970's she was being rebuilt to be returned to long-distance excursion service. Belatedly, photos may be made of G-5's on eastern Long Island.

Construction date	Number	Retired
June, 1929	4207	October, 1955

JOHN KRAUSE

G-5 4-6-0's Nos. 40, 41 and 49 were frequent sprinters on the Greenport runs during the days when the Ten-Wheelers wore round number plates. ABOVE and RIGHT: No. 40 is shown at Greenport on two different occasions in the late 1930's, waiting to take Train No. 211 on the 87-mile trip through the pine barrens of Suffolk and suburbs of Nassau to Jamaica. BELOW: On January 6, 1935, the 40 took a drink of a few thousand gallons from the old, original water tower at Oyster Bay. LEFT: She crosses the high trestle at Kings Park on March 19, 1950. When she was retired, in June, 1952, she was the last of the 40's to go, leaving only 39 and 50 on the roster to represent the dozen G-5's built in 1929.

F. R. DIRKES

Construction date	Number	Retired
June, 1929	4208	June, 1952

F. R. DIRKES

JOHN KRAUSE

ABOVE: On a cold, clear winter day in 1941, G-5 No. 41 left fleecy white billows of exhaust vapor to mark her travels with a pair of old "Ping Pong" round-roof coaches on the Oyster Bay Branch at Sea Cliff. LEFT: On another winter day, seven years later, 41 and sister 38 keep up steam in the Oyster Bay yard. The 39-ton P-54 coaches, so intimately a part of the G-5 era, were nicknamed "Ping Pongs" by LIRR crews, because they were prone to much bouncing and shaking when several of them were coupled between a 120-ton locomotive in front and a string of heavy PRR P-70 coaches behind. The "Pings" were to outlive the steam age by nearly two decades, the last being retired in 1974.

Construction date	Number	Retired
June, 1929	4209	November, 1951

The three photos of No. 42 clearly illustrate the metamorphosis of the G-5 over the years. LEFT: The nine original G-5's had no marker lights on the pilot beam as built, but by 1928-29, when the latter twenty-two were built, their appearance was that of No. 42 at Bethpage Junction in the 1930's, with four-legged classification lamps mounted high on the smokebox, identical-appearing marker lamps on the pilot beam, round number plate and big standard headlight. As built, they also had no cinder shield on the cab roof, or curved baffle behind the whistle. LOWER LEFT: By March 10, 1946, on Cold Spring hill, some obvious changes had begun to appear; the classification lamps had been removed by 1941 and cast-iron keystone number plates—standard on PRR passenger power—had replaced the brass round number plates in 1942. BELOW: At New Hyde Park, shortly before she met her demise, we see the completion of the evolutionary process, with small cylindrical markers on the smokebox and smaller headlight. Fortunately, LIRR engines never suffered the hideous "face-lifting" that many PRR classes received (page 11) when the position of the headlight and generator was reversed and a big platform was mounted on the smokebox front.

F. R. DIRKES

F. R. DIRKES   F. G. ZAHN

Construction date	Number	Retired
June, 1929	4210	November, 1951

42

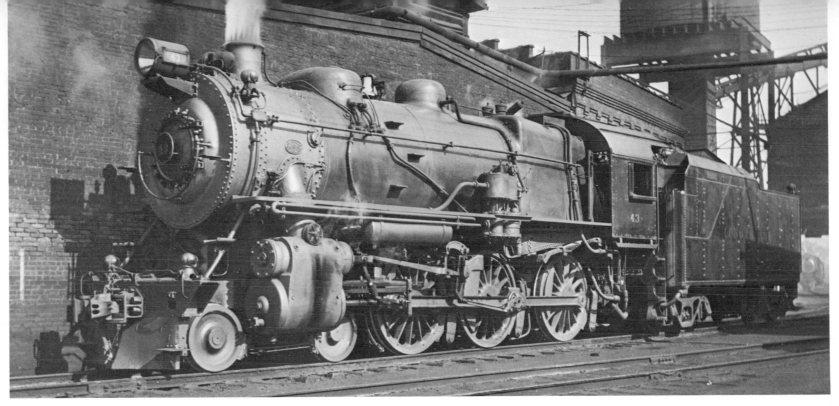

F. R. DIRKES

JOHN KRAUSE

ABOVE: With the steam blower jets on her stack turned on, No. 43 casts her shadow on the end wall of the Morris Park roundhouse on March 27, 1937. LEFT: The engineer leans out of the cab window to give the photographer the once-over, as the 43 and her train clatters through the maze of switches at Jamaica on October 29, 1948. The reasons for the change of marker lamps and headlights so late in the careers of PRR/LIRR steam locomotives are lost in history, some having received the newer equipment as early as 1944 and some never receiving it. No. 45, for example, went to the torch in 1950, with her original big headlight and the four-legged markers intact. Several other G-5's retained their big headlights, including Nos. 24 and 49—the former being the only G-5 to survive until the end of steam in 1955 with the big headlight. By 1947, No. 30 had gotten the small light, but two years later she had a big one again! All of which seems to prove that changing these electrical appliances was totally unnecessary. Although the G-5 was a very successful locomotive design and performed well the tasks assigned to it, there was one major design problem. Since the wide Belpaire firebox had to ride above the rear driving wheels, there was a long space here (8 feet between the centers of the second and third drivers, compared to 6 feet 3 inches between the first and second), which, combined with the lack of a trailing truck, caused severe pounding at high speeds. The resulting rough-riding adversely affected the crewmen, especially the firemen who had to shovel coal by hand on the oscillating deck. The long connecting rod between the second and third drivers also was prone to loosening at high speed. Periodically photos were run in the now-defunct *Long Island Press*, showing the rear driver of a G-5, with the rod hanging down in the shape of a question mark and a caption that began: "Why the commuters were late last night . . ."

Construction date	Number	Retired
July, 1929	4211	November, 1950

ABOVE: Train No. 610, powered by No. 44 at Hicksville in the pre-World War II era. UPPER RIGHT: Among the maladies which plagued the LIRR were washouts after severe storms. On November 17, 1935 No. 44 was pulling the first westbound train from Greenport after a Nor'easter, when she hit a weakened part of the embankment at the Wilson Farm Crossing, near Aquebogue, upsetting the entire train. When G-5 No. 50 was dispatched to tow the 44 back to Jamaica, she was returning a favor, for it was No. 44 which had brought No. 50 in after the latter locomotive was wrecked with the *Cannonball,* the LIRR's crack train, at Montauk in 1932! As built and through the 1930's the center driving wheels of the G-5 class had no flanges, as this picture clearly shows. Apparently this practice, which was devised so the locomotive could negotiate sharp curves, was unnecessary on the LIRR, for the Ten-Wheelers all had flanged rims on their main driving wheels by the 1940's. LOWER RIGHT: Blasting past the semaphores at New Hyde Park in 1947. At 20 years, 11 months of age, No. 44 joined No. 36 in being the two shortest-lived of the 31 LIRR G-5 engines.

Construction date	Number	Retired
July, 1929	4212	June, 1950

F. R. DIRKES

In the year 1940, the United States was rapidly rearming, with total war already raging in Europe and the national interests of Japan and the USA on a collision course in the Pacific Ocean area of the globe. Long Island was to play a vital role in the upcoming conflict, just as it had in the Spanish-American War and in World War I. In both earlier struggles, the LIRR was the premier transportation link that delivered the men and material to the training camps on the Island and later to the ships in New York Harbor. In World War II, the task was greater, however, for major war industries, including Republic Aviation, which built the Air Force's P-47 *Thunderbolt* and Grumman, builder of the Navy's *Wildcat* and *Hellcat* fighters, had located along the LIRR's tracks in the 1930's. The railroad

was prepared, with its fleet of nineteen heavy H-10 2-8-0's and thirty-one G-5 4-6-0's, plus leased Pennsy power—all of a capacity unknown to the Long Island just twenty years earlier. With the reactivation of Camp Upton at Yaphank, G-5 and other classes handled many extra troop movements. ABOVE: No. 45, pulling four baggage cars of equipment and nine coaches packed with soldiers from Camp Upton, crosses New South Road near Hicksville, when Nassau County was still planted in potatoes and rural in character.

Construction date	Number	Retired
July, 1929	4213	August, 1950

F. R. DIRKES

W. S. BOERCKEL

LEFT: Under a billowing canopy of smoke and steam, No. 46 sped Train 236 through Westbury on January 22, 1940. LOWER LEFT: In October of that same year, the 46 traversed the temporary timber trestle which had been erected as a shoo-fly during the rebuilding of the Roslyn Road bridge on the Oyster Bay Branch. BELOW: In 1949, No. 46, nearing the end of her short but useful career, scrutinizes the outside world from her snug stall in the Morris Park roundhouse. The 110P82A tender which arrived with No. 46 when she was new in 1929, survived the locomotive, being the tender assigned to No. 39 when she was selected for preservation.

Construction date	Number	Retired
July, 1929	4214	August, 1950

F. G. ZAHN

F. R. DIRKES

LEFT: No. 47, swinging past B Tower, Bethpage, in 1940. ABOVE: A portrait of the dapper G-5 at Oyster Bay on September 4, 1949. BELOW: A rare photo indeed, as No. 47 pulls a Speonk commuter train through Islip in August, 1948. Although the G-5's were in regular service on the Montauk Branch for a quarter century, very few were photographed operating on that line.

C. V. PARKINSON (ZIEL COLLECTION)

Construction date	Number	Retired
August, 1929	4215	August, 1951

JOHN KRAUSE

HARRY J. TREDE

LEFT: No. 48 races through the woods near Stony Brook with the rider car for the Kings Park Hospital turnaround, in June, 1949. At this time, the LIRR was still extremely smoke-conscious, especially in densely populated Queens County and "Watch Your Stack" signs were posted along the right-of-way. On the eastern branchlines, however, John Krause was one of the very first railway photographers to make "smoke arrangements"—to brief the crew as to where he would be stationed, prior to their departure from the terminal. In later decades pre-ordered smoke became a common practice, but back in 1949, such arrangements were novel, indeed! ABOVE: A few years earlier, No. 48 emerged from under the Ellison Avenue bridge at Westbury. Because of its easy accessibility and the large numbers of railway photographers living in the metropolitan New York region, the Long Island Rail Road—the west end of it, at least—was very well photographed from the 1920's onward. Even dating back into the 1890's, a surprising number of good photos have survived. The result was that engines 20 to 50—the thirty-one G-5 4-6-0's—became perhaps the most photographed class of locomotives of a comparable number in the USA, if not the world. The author's collection of the LIRR G-5's alone, consists of over 650 8 x 10 prints of regular-service (not fantrip) pictures which occupy nine tightly-packed inches of a file drawer and is still growing!

Construction date	Number	Retired
September, 1929	4216	November, 1951

ALBERT BAYLES (ZIEL COLLECTION)

F. R. DIRKES

JOHN KRAUSE

Construction date	Number	Retired
October, 1929	4217	November, 1951

ABOVE LEFT: No. 49 brings an excursion train westbound from Camp Upton through the flatlands of the middle of Long Island, east of Medford on April 28, 1940. ABOVE: Train No. 36 to Speonk rolls along the Montauk Branch at Lynbrook, just after World War II. LEFT: It's that one-car Kings Park turnaround again, whipping up the autumn leaves on the platform as she races through Stony Brook station. The manual-block semaphore in the background was once a common fixture at virtually every station; just two remain in existence, including this one, which is being held by the author for eventual display in a planned museum of LIRR history. Note that the lighting on No. 49 in the two latter photos is from exactly opposite angles.

49

W. J. RUGEN (HUNEKE COLLECTION)

Long Island Rail Road No. 50 was the last G-5 ever built and the newest steam locomotive to be owned by the LIRR, having arrived from Altoona in January, 1930. Like her sisters, No. 50 saw service on all non-electrified branches of the LIRR, but she is best remembered as the Montauk meanderer, for fully half of the known photos of the G-5's east of Babylon depict No. 50! ABOVE: With a corner of the renowned Montauk Manor showing above her tender, the 50 reposes in the weeds at the easternmost terminus of the railroad on August 4, 1935. It was at 6:45 on the evening of October 25, 1932, that No. 50 was bringing the *Cannonball* into Montauk when she jumped the track, piling up the train and killing both enginemen, a mile west of the terminal. The crew had previously reported trouble with the brakes and deteriorating track maintenance in the area was already an issue before the wreck, but the LIRR claimed the crew had exceeded the speed restriction. BELOW: Nos. 50 and 42 relax on Independence Day, 1937 at Speonk, where they will work westbound commuter trains to Jamaica the following morning. The stenciled NL on the pilot beam in these photographs was PRR code for the assignment of locomotives; in this instance New York Region, Long Island. UPPER RIGHT: Between Bay Shore and Brightwaters in 1947, No. 50 churned up the powdery snow with the *Patchogue Scoot,* the local train between Babylon and Patchogue. So rare was the appearance of the G-5 east of Speonk after 1940, that Southampton-raised J. P. Krzenski never saw one until the New York State special exhibit train was spotted at Southampton depot in 1948—with a G-5 as power. "I spent hours in the cab", he reports, "it being my first encounter with this great engine".

C. V. PARKINSON (ZIEL COLLECTION)

BELOW: On October 9, 1955, in the sunset of both the day and of her career, dirty and grimy No. 50, coupled behind No. 39, waited her final calls to duty; to head the last commuter train behind steam the following morning and to briefly power a work train extra the day after that. This terminal at Oyster Bay dispatched the last regular steam trains on the LIRR, powered by Nos. 38, 39 and 50, on Monday morning, October 10th; then came the work train on the 11th. When No. 35 hauled an excursion special the following Sunday, October 16, 1955 (page 19), it was all over—for both the G-5 and twelve decades of steam on the LIRR.

Construction date	Number	Retired
November, 1929	4218	October, 1955

F. R. DIRKES

ART HUNEKE

THE DECLINE OF THE G-5

It is ironic that a locomotive design as successful as the G-5 should have been downgraded so early in its career, but that is precisely what happened to the Long Island members of the family. In June, 1931, when over two-thirds of the G-5 roster was just two or three years old, the "Limited Express" assignment was taken away from the massive Ten-Wheeler when K-4 Pacifics, newly leased from the parent Pennsylvania Railroad, displaced them on the pretigious Montauk "Straw-Hat Limiteds." Thereafter, the G-5 still handled some trains to Montauk and Greenport, but the bigger, heavier expresses—the "name trains"—usually drew a K-4. For the most part, after mid-June of 1931, the LIRR G-5's were pressed back into the prosaic, but vital, role of commuter conveyor and peddler freight mover, more than fate Kiesel had intended for them. Although the K-4 carried just a few tons more per axle than the G-5, the difference necessitated the replacement of the 215-ton bridge over the Shinnecock Canal in Hampton Bays with a massive 800-ton span to accommodate the 4-6-2's at speed. In the two months prior to the bridge replacement, the new one was erected alongside the old and on June 13th, after a G-5 came through with the last train of the evening, the Saturday-only *South Shore Express*, the turn-of-the-century span was slid aside and the new one eased into its place by sand jacks. RIGHT: An LIRR photographer caught the approach of the last train to cross the old bridge; a G-5 with the two parlor cars, combine and two coaches of the *South Shore Express*. Just two weeks later, on June 27th, Charles B. Chaney photographed the *Shinnecock Express*, the *Cannon Ball* and the *South Shore Express*—each rolling behind a big K-4!

A final irony concerning the Long Island G-5: although there is a considerable number of photographs extant of the other classes of locomotives standing derelict at Jamaica awaiting their final journey to the scrapyard, virtually no such pictures exist of the G-5. LEFT: One of the very few photos of the great Ten-Wheeler in final decline shows No. 28, with a sister—probably No. 22—behind, coupled to a derelict old gondola car at Holban Yard in the summer of 1955. Her million-plus miles career as a "local passenger and medium tonnage freight locomotive" now in the receding past, No. 28, minus her number plate, bell, speed control unit, injectors and other reusable parts, spent her last days, forlorn and forgotten. Before the final dispatch to the scrapper, vandals would smash 28's headlight glass and souvenir hunters would remove her builder's plates and whistle. Within a few days she was gone, with only fond memories and fading photographs to mark her three decades of useful service. G-5 No. 28, like her sisters, was taken away from us and we are the poorer for it; never again to thrill to her thunder and fire, her white steam and black smoke, her pungent valve oil odors and lonely whistle in the crisp winter night, as in days so long gone, when she highballed through the pine barrens and villages and past the little Victorian stations of Long Island.

51

On Saturday, October 8, 1955, with "Hot-Rod" McCann at the throttle, topping 80 mph on his last steam run, No. 35 deadheaded a single brand-new coach to Riverhead where she headed back west with a load of Boy Scouts. No. 39, with a similar consist of Scouts, traveled east from Jamaica. The two engines, their smokebox and cylinder saddle fronts painted a garish silver for the occasion, met at Hicksville, where "end of steam" ceremonies were held in the rain. The steam era officially ended, a pair of newly arrived Alco RS-3 diesels which were replacing the last steamers, coupled onto the rear of the coaches and returned to the originating stations. LEFT: Coupled nose-to-nose, the 35 and 39 chugged through Mineola, en route back to Jamaica. Nobody could have forseen, that gray dismal October day, that this, the presumably last movement of two live steam engines on the Long Island Rail Road, was amazingly prophetic. Not only were these the only LIRR locomotives to be later preserved, but at a distant date, at least a quarter-century later, the pair could well be teamed up again—both with hot fires on their grates and steam producing horsepower in their cylinders!

G-5 PRESERVATION AND RESTORATION

When the railways retired their last steam locomotives, many, including the Long Island Rail Road, donated engines to museums and municipalities for display. James A. Shultz, public relations officer under LIRR President Thomas M. Goodfellow and creator of "Dashing Dan," when queried concerning the rationale of saving G-5's No. 35 and No. 39 from the scrapper's torch, related "Tom was no historian and had no interest in steam. Few of us did, but I convinced him that as scrap, the engines were worth $5000 each, but we could get $10,000 worth of good free publicity by giving them away. We offered one to

BELOW: No. 35 had to be extensively dismantled right at the display site before she was loaded onto the truck that returned her to LIRR tracks in June, 1978. RIGHT: On April 23, 1977, volunteers were removing the boiler jacketing and sealing the throttle in the steam dome of No. 39, preparatory to a hydrostatic test which was done right on the Museum grounds.

Nassau County and one to Suffolk. Nassau accepted, but Suffolk had no interest. Ward Melville heard of the offer and said that he would like to display an engine at the Carriage House Museum in Stony Brook. We gave him Suffolk's locomotive."

As the last G-5's and H-10's were being readied for disposal to the scrap merchant, one of the officials of the Mechanical Department called Goodfellow to find out which two engines to save. "Just save the two in best shape," was the reply. Since 35 and 39 had been spruced up for the final "decommissioning cere-

monies" a few weeks previously, they were the ones chosen. A poor choice, since the logical selection would have been one G-5 and one H-10, rather than two of the same class. Since No. 50 was the last steamer built for the LIRR, she was the one that should have been preserved. If the choice had to be two G-5's, one should have been No. 21 or 24—the pair from the early series that survived until the end of steam. Instead, two identical engines of the 1928-29 batch were chosen.

Coincidentally, both No. 35 and No. 39 were put on display at the same time—June, 1956; negotiations for their release by two different organizations working completely independently began at the same time—Spring, 1975; and the heavy work of preparing both engines for movement commenced at the same time—early in 1977. There the similarity ends, for the Black River & Western Railroad, in the Delaware River Valley of western New Jersey, has leased No. 35 from Nassau County for twenty years to operate on their shortline. The Museums At Stony Brook has given No. 39 to The Steam Locomotive 39 Preservation Fund which, along with The Main Line Steam Foundation, is going to rebuild and operate her in excursion service on the main tracks of her native LIRR. It is hoped that the pair will be brought together for doubleheaders both on and off Long Island.

There is much cause for celebration, but had it not been for the public relations ideas of Jim Schultz, nothing would have been saved. All the thousands of people who will ride behind both locomotives through the 1980's and beyond owe him a heartfelt "Thank you" for helping preserve the LONG ISLAND HERITAGE.